WORM FARMING HANDBOOK

A Comprehensive Guide to Sustainable Vermiculture for Beginners and Experts

Chad R. Weaver

Copyright © Chad R. Weaver, 2024.

All rights reserved. No part of this publication may be reproduced, distributed or transmitted in any form or by any means, including photocopying, recording or other electronic or mechanical methods, without the prior written permission of the publisher, except in the case of brief quotations embodied in critical reviews and certain other noncommercial uses permitted by copyright law.

Table of content

CHAPTER ONE 7
INTRODUCTION TO WORM FARMING 7
- 1.1 What is Worm Farming? 7
- 1.2 Benefits of Worm Farming 7
- 1.3 Overview of the Worm Farming Process 8

CHAPTER TWO 9
UNDERSTANDING WORMS 9
- 2.1 Types of Worms Used in Vermiculture 9
- 2.2 Anatomy and Biology of Composting Worms 9
- 2.3 Worm Behavior and Life Cycle 10

CHAPTER THREE 12
SETTING UP YOUR WORM FARM 12
- 3.1 Choosing the Right Worm Bin 12
- 3.2 Preparing the Bedding 12
- 3.3 Sourcing and Introducing Your Worms 13
- 3.4 Optimal Conditions for Worm Farming 14

CHAPTER FOUR 19
FEEDING YOUR WORMS 19
- 4.1 What to Feed Your Worms 19
- 4.2 Foods to Avoid 20
- 4.3 Creating a Feeding Schedule 20
- 4.4 Managing Food Waste 21

CHAPTER FIVE 23
MAINTAINING YOUR WORM FARM 23
5.1 Monitoring Moisture Levels 23
5.2 Temperature Control...23
5.3 Aeration and Oxygenation 24
5.4 Dealing with Pests and Problems 25

CHAPTER SIX 27
HARVESTING WORM CASTINGS 27
6.1 When to Harvest 27
6.2 Methods of Harvesting Worm Castings 27
6.3 Storing and Using Worm Castings 29

CHAPTER SEVEN 31
WORM REPRODUCTION AND GROWTH 31
7.1 Breeding Worms 31
7.2 Managing Worm Population...............................32
7.3 Expanding Your Worm Farm 33

CHAPTER EIGHT ADVANCED WORM FARMING TECHNIQUES 36
8.1 Indoor vs. Outdoor Worm Farming 36
8.2 Using Worm Towers and Trench Systems 37
8.3 Integrating Worm Farming with Other Systems .39

CHAPTER NINE..42
COMMERCIAL WORM FARMING...........................42
9.1 Scaling Up Your Worm Farm..............................42

9.2 Marketing and Selling Worm Castings................43

9.3 Diversifying Your Worm Products......................45

CHAPTER TEN 47

TROUBLESHOOTING COMMON ISSUES...............47

10.1 Identifying and Solving Common Problems 47

10.2 Preventing Worm Farm Failures 49

10.3 Tips from Experienced Worm Farmers 50

CHAPTER ELEVEN...52

SUSTAINABLE PRACTICES IN WORM FARMING
....52

11.1 Environmental Benefits 52

11.2 Sustainable Waste Management 53

11.3 Community Worm Farming Initiatives 54

CHAPTER TWELVE..56

CASE STUDIES AND SUCCESS STORIES 56

12.1 Profiles of Successful Worm Farmers 56

12.2 Lessons Learned from Real-life Experiences 58

CHAPTER THIRTEEN...61

RESOURCES AND FURTHER READING 61

13.1 Recommended Books and Websites..................61

13.2 Organizations and Associations........................63

13.3 Glossary of Terms...64

CHAPTER FOURTEEN 66

APPENDICES 66

14.1 Frequently Asked Questions (FAQ) 66

14.2 Templates and Record-Keeping Forms 68

14.3 Supplier Directory 69

CHAPTER FIFTEEN 72

INDEX 72

CHAPTER ONE

INTRODUCTION TO WORM FARMING

1.1 What is Worm Farming?

Worm farming, also known as vermiculture or vermicomposting, involves the cultivation of worms to decompose organic waste into nutrient-rich compost. This practice not only helps in recycling kitchen and garden waste but also produces valuable worm castings, which can be used to enrich soil.

1.2 Benefits of Worm Farming

- **Environmental Impact:** Reduces landfill waste and greenhouse gas emissions.

-**Soil Health:** Produces worm castings that improve soil structure, aeration, and nutrient content.

- **Sustainable Waste Management:** Provides an eco-friendly method to dispose of organic waste.

-**Cost-Effective:** Lowers the need for chemical fertilizers and soil conditioners.

-**Educational Value:** Offers a hands-on learning experience about ecosystems and sustainability.

1.3 Overview of the Worm Farming Process

-Setting Up: Choose an appropriate worm bin, prepare bedding, and introduce the worms.

-Feeding: Provide the worms with suitable food scraps and maintain a feeding schedule.

-Maintenance: Regularly monitor and adjust moisture, temperature, and aeration levels.

-Harvesting: Collect worm castings for use as compost and manage worm population for continuous farming.

-Advanced Techniques: Explore methods such as worm towers, trench systems, and integrating vermiculture with other sustainable practices.

CHAPTER TWO

UNDERSTANDING WORMS

2.1 Types of Worms Used in Vermiculture

- **Red Wigglers (Eisenia fetida):** The most commonly used worms in vermiculture, known for their rapid reproduction and high composting efficiency.

- **European Nightcrawlers (Eisenia hortensis):** Larger than red wigglers, these worms are suitable for both composting and as fishing bait.

-**African Nightcrawlers (Eudrilus eugeniae):** Known for their ability to break down tough organic material quickly, thriving in warmer climates.

-**Blue Worms (Perionyx excavatus):** Effective composters in tropical and subtropical regions, known for their rapid growth and reproduction rates.

2.2 Anatomy and Biology of Composting Worms

-**External Anatomy:** Features include the clitellum (a thickened, glandular section used in reproduction), segments, setae (tiny bristles), and the mouth and anus.

-Internal Anatomy: Includes the digestive system (mouth, pharynx, esophagus, crop, gizzard, intestine), circulatory system (closed system with dorsal and ventral blood vessels), and nervous system (simple brain and nerve cord).

-Reproductive System: Hermaphroditic worms possess both male and female reproductive organs, with the clitellum playing a key role in the exchange of sperm and cocoon formation.

2.3 Worm Behavior and Life Cycle

-Behavior: Worms are sensitive to light and vibrations, preferring dark, moist environments. They consume organic matter by ingesting it and digesting it with the help of microorganisms in their gut.

-Life Cycle:

  -Egg Stage: Worms lay cocoons containing multiple eggs, which hatch in about 3 weeks.

  -Juvenile Stage: Newly hatched worms are small, pale, and lack a clitellum. They mature over a period of 8-10 weeks.

  -Adult Stage: Mature worms develop a clitellum and can reproduce, laying cocoons every 7-10 days under optimal conditions. Worms can live for several years, continuously producing castings and reproducing.

CHAPTER THREE

SETTING UP YOUR WORM FARM

3.1 Choosing the Right Worm Bin

-Types of Bins:

-Plastic Bins: Affordable and widely available, but require proper ventilation.

- Wooden Bins: Naturally aerated and absorbent, but may degrade over time.

-Commercially Made Bins: Designed specifically for worm farming with features like stackable trays and drainage systems.

-Size and Capacity: Consider the amount of organic waste you generate to determine the appropriate size of the bin.

-Ventilation and Drainage: Ensure the bin has adequate airflow and a way to manage excess moisture to prevent anaerobic conditions.

3.2 Preparing the Bedding

-Materials:

-Shredded Paper: Newspaper, office paper, and cardboard (ensure ink is non-toxic).

-Coconut Coir: A sustainable option that retains moisture well.

-Peat Moss: Commonly used, but less sustainable due to environmental concerns.

-Compost or Aged Manure: Adds beneficial microorganisms to the bedding.

- Preparation Steps:

-Shredding: Break down large pieces of bedding material.

-Moistening: Soak the bedding materials in water until they are as damp as a wrung-out sponge.

-Mixing: Combine different types of bedding to create a balanced environment.

-Filling the Bin: Add the bedding to the bin to a depth of 6-8 inches.

3.3 Sourcing and Introducing Your Worms

-Sourcing Worms:

- **Reputable Suppliers:** Purchase worms from established vermiculture businesses to ensure healthy stock.

- **Local Sources:** Consider local garden centers or community worm farmers.

-Introducing Worms:

- Acclimatization: Allow worms to adjust to their new environment by spreading them evenly over the prepared bedding.

- Initial Feeding: Provide a small amount of food to start, gradually increasing as the worms settle in.

- Monitoring: Observe the worms for the first few days to ensure they are burrowing and showing signs of healthy activity.

3.4 Optimal Conditions for Worm Farming

-Temperature:

- Ideal Range: 55°F to 77°F (13°C to 25°C).

-Effects of Temperature:

- Too Cold: Slows down worm activity and reproduction; temperatures below 40°F (4°C) can be fatal.

-Too Hot: Causes stress, dehydration, and can be fatal if temperatures exceed 85°F (29°C).

-Management Tips:

- Keep the bin in a temperature-controlled environment.

- Insulate the bin in colder climates.

- Provide shade and increase ventilation in warmer climates.

-Moisture:

-Ideal Moisture Level: Bedding should be as damp as a wrung-out sponge (70-90% moisture content).

-Effects of Moisture:

-Too Dry: Worms dehydrate, reducing activity and reproduction.

-Too Wet: Creates anaerobic conditions, leading to bad odors and potential worm death.

-Management Tips:

- Regularly check and adjust moisture levels.

- Add water if bedding is dry, or add dry bedding if it's too wet.

- Ensure proper drainage to avoid water accumulation at the bottom of the bin.

- pH Levels:

-Ideal pH Range: 6.0 to 7.0.

-Effects of pH:

-Too Acidic: Can cause skin irritation and harm worms.

-Too Alkaline: Can lead to ammonia build-up, which is toxic to worms.

-Management Tips:

- Monitor pH levels regularly using a pH meter or test strips.

- Add crushed eggshells or agricultural lime to neutralize acidity.

- Avoid adding highly acidic foods like citrus fruits in large quantities.

-Aeration:

-Importance: Worms need oxygen to survive and thrive.

-Management Tips:

- Fluff and turn the bedding regularly to maintain airflow.

- Ensure the bin has adequate ventilation holes.

- Avoid compacting the bedding with too much food waste at once.

- Light:

-Sensitivity: Worms are sensitive to light and prefer dark environments.

-Management Tips:

- Keep the worm bin in a shaded area.

- Cover the bin with a breathable fabric or lid to block light while maintaining airflow.

-Food and Feeding:

-Diet: Provide a balanced mix of organic waste including fruit and vegetable scraps, coffee grounds, tea bags, and crushed eggshells.

-Avoid: Meat, dairy, oily foods, spicy foods, and large amounts of citrus.

-Feeding Frequency: Feed small amounts regularly, observing how quickly the worms consume the food.

-Management Tips:

- Chop food scraps into small pieces to facilitate decomposition.

- Monitor and adjust feeding amounts based on worm activity and consumption rates.

CHAPTER FOUR

FEEDING YOUR WORMS

4.1 What to Feed Your Worms

-Suitable Foods:

  -Fruit Scraps: Apple cores, banana peels, melon rinds, etc.

  -Vegetable Scraps: Lettuce leaves, potato peels, carrot tops, etc.

  -Grains: Cooked rice, pasta, bread (in moderation).

  -Coffee Grounds and Filters: A good source of nitrogen.

  -Tea Bags and Leaves: Remove any staples from tea bags.

  -Crushed Eggshells: Adds calcium and helps balance pH.

  -Paper Products: Shredded newspaper, cardboard, and paper towels.

-Preparation Tips:

  -Chop or blend scraps into small pieces to speed up decomposition.

  -Avoid adding large quantities of any single type of food at once.

4.2 Foods to Avoid

-Meat and Dairy: Attract pests and create odors.

-Oily and Greasy Foods: Difficult for worms to break down.

-Spicy Foods: Can irritate worms.

-Citrus Fruits: High acidity can harm worms.

-Processed Foods: Often contain preservatives and additives that are harmful to worms.

-Large Quantities of Onion and Garlic: Can be too pungent and acidic.

4.3 Creating a Feeding Schedule

-Frequency:

  -Feed your worms once or twice a week.

  - Start with small amounts and adjust based on how quickly the worms consume the food.

-Observation:

  - Check the bin regularly to see how much food remains.

- Adjust feeding frequency and quantity based on consumption rates.

-Quantity:

- Rule of thumb: worms can eat about half their weight in food per day.

- For a pound of worms, start with ½ pound of food per day.

-Record Keeping:

- Maintain a feeding log to track amounts and types of food added.

-Note any changes in worm activity or bin conditions.

4.4 Managing Food Waste

-Pre-Composting:

- Pre-composting food scraps for a few days can speed up decomposition.

- Store scraps in a sealed container to avoid odors and pests.

-Avoid Overfeeding:

- Overfeeding can lead to excess moisture and odors.

- Ensure all food is consumed before adding more.

-Balance:

-Maintain a balance of green (nitrogen-rich) and brown (carbon-rich) materials.

-Greens: fruit and vegetable scraps, coffee grounds.

- Browns: shredded paper, cardboard, dried leaves.

-Troubleshooting:

-Odors: Caused by overfeeding or anaerobic conditions; reduce food input and aerate bedding.

-Pests: Attracted by certain foods; avoid meats, dairy, and oily foods, and ensure proper bin hygiene.

-Mold and Mildew: Can appear if food is not consumed quickly; reduce feeding and remove moldy food if necessary.

CHAPTER FIVE

MAINTAINING YOUR WORM FARM

5.1 Monitoring Moisture Levels

-Ideal Moisture: Bedding should be as damp as a wrung-out sponge (70-90% moisture content).

-Monitoring Techniques:

  -Manual Check: Squeeze a handful of bedding; it should feel moist but not dripping.

  -Moisture Meters: Use a moisture meter for more precise measurements.

-Adjusting Moisture:

  -Too Dry: Sprinkle water over the bedding or add moistened bedding materials.

  -Too Wet: Add dry bedding such as shredded newspaper or cardboard. Ensure proper drainage and aeration to remove excess moisture.

5.2 Temperature Control

-Ideal Temperature Range: 55°F to 77°F (13°C to 25°C).

-Managing Temperature:

-Cold Climates: Insulate the bin, use heating pads designed for worm bins, or move the bin indoors.

-Hot Climates: Keep the bin in a shaded area, provide ventilation, and add frozen water bottles wrapped in cloth to cool the bin.

-Monitoring Temperature:

-Thermometer: Use a soil thermometer to regularly check the bin's internal temperature.

-Signs of Stress: Worms climbing the sides of the bin or trying to escape can indicate temperature issues.

5.3 Aeration and Oxygenation

-Importance: Worms need oxygen for respiration; aerated bedding prevents anaerobic conditions.

-Aeration Techniques:

-Fluffing Bedding: Turn and fluff the bedding regularly to maintain airflow.

-Ventilation: Ensure the bin has adequate ventilation holes. Avoid over-packing the bin with food or bedding.

-Layering: Alternate layers of food and bedding to create air pockets.

-Avoid Compaction: Don't add too much food at once, and regularly check for areas that might be compacted.

5.4 Dealing with Pests and Problems

-Common Pests:

  -Fruit Flies: Avoid overfeeding, cover food with bedding, and use traps if necessary.

  -Ants: Ensure the bin is moist but not waterlogged, use barriers or diatomaceous earth around the bin.

  -Mites: Usually harmless, but can be reduced by keeping the bin dry and adding lime or crushed eggshells.

-Problem Signs and Solutions:

  -Odors: Caused by overfeeding or anaerobic conditions. Solution: reduce feeding, aerate bedding, and ensure proper drainage.

  -Worms Trying to Escape: Indicates poor conditions such as extreme temperatures, low oxygen, or high acidity. Solution: adjust temperature, increase aeration, and check pH levels.

-Mold and Mildew: Appear if food is not consumed quickly. Solution: reduce feeding, remove moldy food, and ensure proper aeration.

-Unhealthy Worms: Look for signs like lethargy or discolored worms. Solution: check and optimize moisture, temperature, pH levels, and feeding habits.

CHAPTER SIX

HARVESTING WORM CASTINGS

6.1 When to Harvest

-Signs It's Time to Harvest:

-Color and Texture: Castings look like dark, crumbly soil.

-Volume: The bin becomes full, and bedding material is no longer recognizable.

-Timeframe: Generally, harvesting is needed every 3-6 months, depending on the worm population and feeding rate.

-Observations:

-Worm Activity: Worms may migrate to fresher bedding or food layers, indicating castings are ready to be harvested.

-Odor: A healthy bin with ready castings should have an earthy smell, not foul odors.

6.2 Methods of Harvesting Worm Castings

-Manual Sorting:

-Step-by-Step:

1. Spread a tarp or plastic sheet.

2. Dump the contents of the bin onto the tarp.

3. Create small mounds of compost.

4. Wait for worms to burrow away from light, then collect the top layer of castings.

5. Repeat until most worms are separated.

- Light Method:

  -Step-by-Step:

1. Place small piles of compost under bright light.

2. Worms will move away from the light to the bottom of the piles.

3. Gradually remove the top layer of castings, re-piling as needed until mostly worms remain.

-Migration Method:

  -Step-by-Step:

1. Move food scraps to one side of the bin.

2. Wait a week for worms to migrate to the new food source.

3. Harvest castings from the side without fresh food.

-Sifting Method:

-Step-by-Step:

1. Use a sieve or screen with appropriate mesh size.

2. Place compost on the screen and shake to separate castings from worms and larger debris.

6.3 Storing and Using Worm Castings

-Storing Castings:

-Containers: Store in breathable bags or containers to prevent moisture buildup and mold.

-Location: Keep in a cool, dark place to maintain nutrient levels.

-Shelf Life: Use within 6 months for best results, although properly stored castings can last longer.

-Using Castings:

-Soil Amendment: Mix with garden soil or potting mix at a ratio of 1:4 for improved soil structure and fertility.

-Top Dressing: Sprinkle directly on the surface of garden beds or potted plants.

-Compost Tea: Brew by soaking castings in water (e.g., 1 cup of castings in 5 gallons of water) for 24-48 hours, then use as a liquid fertilizer.

-Seed Starting Mix: Combine with sand and coconut coir or peat moss for a nutrient-rich seed starting medium.

CHAPTER SEVEN

WORM REPRODUCTION AND GROWTH

7.1 Breeding Worms

-Reproductive Biology:

-Hermaphroditic Nature: Worms possess both male and female reproductive organs, allowing them to mate with any mature worm.

-Clitellum: A thickened, glandular section used in reproduction, becomes more prominent in mature worms.

-Breeding Conditions:

-Optimal Environment: Maintain ideal moisture (70-90%), temperature (55°F to 77°F), and pH (6.0 to 7.0).

-Adequate Food Supply: Provide a steady supply of food to support reproduction and growth.

-Cocoon Production:

-Mating Process: Worms exchange sperm and produce cocoons containing eggs.

- Cocoon Development: Each cocoon can contain 2-5 baby worms and takes about 3 weeks to hatch under optimal conditions.

-Increasing Breeding Efficiency:

- High-Quality Bedding: Use nutrient-rich, moist bedding materials.

- Feeding Regimen: Regular, balanced feeding to support worm health and reproduction.

- Minimizing Stress: Avoid disturbances and maintain stable environmental conditions.

7.2 Managing Worm Population

-Monitoring Population Growth:

- Population Checks: Regularly inspect the worm bin to assess worm density and overall health.

- Signs of Overcrowding: Worms attempting to escape, reduced reproduction rates, and increased competition for food.

-Balancing Population:

- Harvesting Mature Worms: Remove mature worms periodically to reduce overcrowding.

-Dividing the Bin: Split the worm population and material into additional bins when space becomes limited.

-Adjusting Food Supply: Increase food amounts to support a growing population, but avoid overfeeding.

-Dealing with Population Declines:

-Identifying Causes: Check for environmental stressors such as extreme temperatures, improper moisture levels, or poor food quality.

-Remediation Steps: Correct environmental conditions, improve food quality, and remove any dead worms or pests.

7.3 Expanding Your Worm Farm

-Scaling Up:

-Additional Bins: Add new worm bins to increase capacity and accommodate growing worm populations.

-Larger Systems: Transition to larger vermiculture systems, such as continuous flow-through bins or outdoor worm beds.

-Integrating New Techniques:

-Worm Towers: Install worm towers directly in garden beds for localized composting.

-Trench Systems: Dig trenches filled with organic material and worms to compost directly in the garden.

-Maintaining New Systems:

-Consistent Monitoring: Regularly check all bins or systems for optimal conditions.

-Efficient Workflow: Develop a routine for feeding, harvesting, and maintaining multiple systems.

-Resource Management:

-Balanced Inputs: Ensure a steady supply of organic waste to feed expanding worm populations.

-Space Considerations: Allocate adequate space for additional bins or outdoor systems.

- Economic Expansion:

-Commercial Vermiculture: Consider commercial-scale worm farming to produce and sell castings, worms, and other vermiculture products.

-Marketing and Sales: Develop marketing strategies to sell worm castings, compost tea, and live worms to gardeners, farmers, and fishing enthusiasts.

CHAPTER EIGHT
ADVANCED WORM FARMING TECHNIQUES

8.1 Indoor vs. Outdoor Worm Farming

-Indoor Worm Farming:

  -Advantages:

   - Controlled Environment: Easier to maintain optimal temperature and moisture levels.

   -Protection from Elements: Avoids extreme weather conditions, predators, and pests.

   -Convenience: Allows year-round composting and easier monitoring.

  -Challenges:

   -Space Limitations: Indoor bins may be limited by available space.

   -Odor and Pests: Requires diligent maintenance to prevent odors and household pests.

-Outdoor Worm Farming:

  -Advantages:

-Larger Scale: More space for larger bins or systems, allowing for greater composting capacity.

- Natural Conditions: Worms can thrive in a natural environment with less need for intervention.

-Challenges:

- Weather Dependence: Requires management of temperature and moisture to protect worms from extreme conditions.

-Predators and Pests: Greater risk of predation by birds, rodents, and insects.

-Hybrid Systems: Combining indoor and outdoor setups can optimize space and resources, utilizing indoor bins during harsh weather and outdoor systems when conditions are favorable.

8.2 Using Worm Towers and Trench Systems

-Worm Towers:

-Design: Vertical tubes or pipes inserted into garden beds, filled with worms and organic waste.

-Benefits:

- Localized Composting: Directly enriches soil around the tower with worm castings.

- Easy Maintenance: Simple to set up and maintain with minimal disturbance to garden plants.

- Implementation:

  - Drill holes in a PVC pipe or use a large flower pot with holes.

  - Bury part of the tower in the soil, fill with bedding and worms, and regularly add food scraps.

- Trench Systems:

  - Design: Dig trenches in the garden or field, filled with organic waste and worms.

  - Benefits:

    - Large-Scale Composting: Suitable for larger gardens or farming operations.

    - Soil Improvement: Enhances soil fertility and structure over a wide area.

  - Implementation:

    - Dig a trench 12-18 inches deep.

- Layer organic waste and bedding, add worms, and cover with soil.

- Gradually move the trench along the garden bed as each section is processed.

8.3 Integrating Worm Farming with Other Systems

- Aquaponics:

-Synergy: Combine vermiculture with aquaponics to create a closed-loop system where fish waste feeds plants, and worms compost organic matter.

-Benefits:

-Nutrient Recycling: Worm castings can be used to fertilize plants in the aquaponics system.

-Waste Reduction: Composting fish waste and plant trimmings helps manage organic waste.

-Implementation:

- Place worm bins or towers near the aquaponics setup.

- Use compost tea or worm castings to supplement plant nutrients.

- **Permaculture:**

  -Principles: Incorporate worm farming into permaculture designs to enhance soil health and biodiversity.

  -Benefits:

  -Sustainable Practices: Worm farming aligns with permaculture ethics of earth care, people care, and fair share.

  -Soil Enrichment: Improves soil fertility and structure, supporting diverse plant systems.

  - Implementation:

  - Integrate worm bins, towers, or trench systems into permaculture zones.

  - Use worm castings to fertilize food forests, vegetable gardens, and other permaculture areas.

-Gardening and Farming:

  -Application: Use worm farming to enhance traditional gardening and farming practices.

  - Benefits:

- **Improved Crop Yields**: Worm castings provide essential nutrients for plant growth.

- **Sustainable Waste Management**: Reduces reliance on chemical fertilizers and minimizes waste.

- **Implementation**:

- Regularly apply worm castings to garden beds and farm fields.

- Incorporate vermiculture practices into crop rotation and soil management plans.

CHAPTER NINE
COMMERCIAL WORM FARMING

9.1 Scaling Up Your Worm Farm

-Assessing Demand:

  -Market Research: Identify potential customers, including local gardeners, farmers, nurseries, and organic farming communities.

  -Demand Analysis: Evaluate the level of demand for worm castings and other vermiculture products in your region.

-Infrastructure Expansion:

  -Larger Bins or Beds: Invest in larger worm bins, continuous flow-through systems, or outdoor worm beds to increase production capacity.

  -Facility Setup: Ensure your facility can handle increased volumes of organic waste, bedding materials, and worms.

  -Automation: Consider automating processes such as feeding, harvesting, and monitoring environmental conditions to enhance efficiency.

-Labor Management:

-Hiring Help: As you scale up, consider hiring additional labor to manage daily operations, from feeding and harvesting to packaging and sales.

-Training: Provide comprehensive training to ensure workers understand best practices in worm farming and product handling.

-Quality Control:

-Consistency: Implement quality control measures to ensure the consistency and quality of your worm castings and other products.

-Record Keeping: Maintain detailed records of production processes, environmental conditions, and output to monitor and improve efficiency.

9.2 Marketing and Selling Worm Castings

- Brand Development:

-Brand Identity: Create a strong brand identity with a memorable name, logo, and packaging that reflects your commitment to sustainability and quality.

-Marketing Materials: Develop informative and attractive marketing materials, including brochures, labels, and a website.

-Sales Channels:

-Local Markets: Sell directly to customers at farmers markets, garden centers, and local shops.

-Online Sales: Set up an online store to reach a broader audience, using platforms like Etsy, eBay, or your own website.

-Bulk Sales: Establish partnerships with local farms, nurseries, and landscaping companies for bulk sales.

-Promotional Strategies:

-Educational Workshops: Host workshops and demonstrations to educate potential customers about the benefits of worm castings.

-Social Media: Use social media platforms to share success stories, customer testimonials, and educational content.

-Partnerships: Collaborate with local gardening clubs, schools, and community gardens to promote your products.

-**Pricing:**

  -Competitive Pricing: Research local and online prices for worm castings and set competitive prices that reflect the quality of your product.

  -Discounts and Bundles: Offer discounts for bulk purchases or bundle products (e.g., castings and worm tea) to increase sales.

9.3 Diversifying Your Worm Products

-**Worm Tea:**

  -Production: Brew worm tea by soaking worm castings in water (e.g., 1 cup of castings in 5 gallons of water) for 24-48 hours, aerating the mixture to enhance microbial activity.

  -Benefits: Market worm tea as a liquid fertilizer that provides immediate nutrients to plants and enhances soil health.

  -Packaging: Bottle worm tea in various sizes, ensuring proper labeling and instructions for use.

- **Live Worms:**

  -Sales Market: Sell live worms for composting, fishing, or pet food markets.

  -Breeding and Harvesting: Manage breeding programs to ensure a steady supply of healthy worms.

  -Shipping and Handling: Develop safe and effective methods for packaging and shipping live worms to minimize stress and mortality.

-**Additional Products:**

  -Worm Bins: Manufacture and sell worm bins or kits that include everything needed to start a worm farm.

  -Educational Materials: Create and sell books, guides, or online courses on worm farming and vermiculture.

  -Organic Fertilizers: Develop and sell other organic soil amendments and fertilizers derived from worm farming by-products.

CHAPTER TEN

TROUBLESHOOTING COMMON ISSUES

10.1 Identifying and Solving Common Problems

- Moisture Issues:

-Too Dry: Worms become sluggish and bedding feels dry.

-Solution: Add water gradually and mix in moist bedding materials like shredded paper or coconut coir.

-Too Wet: Bedding is soggy, and there may be unpleasant odors.

- Solution: Add dry bedding, ensure proper drainage, and reduce the amount of high-moisture foods.

-Temperature Fluctuations:

-Too Cold: Worms slow down, and composting activity decreases.

-Solution: Insulate the bin, move it to a warmer location, or use a heating pad designed for worm farms.

-Too Hot: Worms try to escape, and bedding may dry out.

-Solution: Move the bin to a cooler, shaded area and ensure proper ventilation.

-Pests and Predators:

-Fruit Flies: Attracted to exposed food.

-Solution: Cover food scraps with bedding and use fruit fly traps if necessary.

-Ants: Invade dry bins.

-Solution: Maintain moisture levels and use barriers like diatomaceous earth around the bin.

-Mites: Can overpopulate in moist conditions.

-Solution: Keep the bin balanced and add lime or crushed eggshells to reduce acidity.

-Odor Problems:

-Rotting Smell: Indicates anaerobic conditions or overfeeding.

-Solution: Turn and aerate the bedding, reduce feeding, and remove any excess or decomposing food.

-Ammonia Smell: Often due to too much nitrogen-rich food.

-Solution: Balance with carbon-rich bedding materials like shredded cardboard or paper.

10.2 Preventing Worm Farm Failures

-Regular Maintenance:

-Routine Checks: Monitor moisture, temperature, and worm activity regularly.

-Balanced Feeding: Avoid overfeeding and maintain a proper balance of green (nitrogen) and brown (carbon) materials.

- Environmental Stability:

-Consistent Conditions: Keep the bin in a stable environment, avoiding extreme temperatures and humidity fluctuations.

-Proper Aeration: Ensure adequate ventilation and avoid compacting the bedding.

-Healthy Worm Population:

-Avoid Overcrowding: Regularly harvest mature worms and expand to additional bins if necessary.

-Disease Prevention: Maintain a clean bin and remove any sick or dead worms promptly.

- **Education and Adaptation:**

  -Continuous Learning: Stay informed about best practices and new techniques in vermiculture.

  -Adaptation: Be willing to adjust methods based on observations and experiences.

10.3 Tips from Experienced Worm Farmers

- Start Small and Scale Up: Begin with a manageable size bin to learn the basics before expanding.

-Feed Consistently but Moderately: Regular feeding helps maintain an active worm population, but avoid overwhelming the bin.

-Use Diverse Bedding Materials: Mix different types of bedding to create a healthy, balanced environment.

-Harvest Regularly: Regularly collect worm castings to prevent overcrowding and maintain optimal conditions.

-Observe and Adjust: Pay attention to your worms and bin conditions, and be ready to make changes as needed.

-Network with Other Farmers: Join local or online worm farming communities to share experiences and solutions.

CHAPTER ELEVEN

SUSTAINABLE PRACTICES IN WORM FARMING

11.1 Environmental Benefits

-Soil Health Improvement:

-Nutrient-Rich Castings: Worm castings enhance soil fertility by providing essential nutrients and beneficial microorganisms.

-Soil Structure: Improves soil aeration and water retention, promoting healthier plant growth.

-Reduction in Landfill Waste:

-Organic Waste Diversion: Composting kitchen scraps and garden waste with worms significantly reduces the amount of organic material sent to landfills.

-Methane Reduction: Decreasing organic waste in landfills lowers methane emissions, a potent greenhouse gas.

-Biodiversity Enhancement:

-Microbial Diversity: Worm farming promotes a diverse microbial ecosystem, beneficial for soil health and plant growth.

-Habitat Creation: Provides habitat and food for beneficial soil organisms, contributing to overall biodiversity.

11.2 Sustainable Waste Management

-Household Waste Reduction:

  -Composting at Home: Encourages households to manage their organic waste sustainably, reducing the burden on municipal waste management systems.

  -Waste Awareness: Promotes awareness and responsibility for waste generation and disposal.

-Circular Economy:

  -Resource Recovery: Transforms waste into valuable products like worm castings and compost tea, closing the loop in the waste cycle.

  -Sustainable Practices: Encourages practices that align with sustainable development goals, reducing reliance on chemical fertilizers and enhancing soil health naturally.

-Industrial and Agricultural Applications:

  -Large-Scale Composting: Integrates vermiculture into industrial and agricultural waste management, handling larger volumes of organic waste.

-Soil Remediation: Utilizes worm castings in soil remediation projects to restore contaminated or degraded soils.

11.3 Community Worm Farming Initiatives

-Educational Programs:

-Schools and Universities: Incorporate worm farming into educational curriculums to teach students about ecology, sustainability, and waste management.

-Workshops and Seminars: Host community workshops to educate the public on the benefits and techniques of worm farming.

-Community Gardens:

-Local Collaboration: Establish worm farms in community gardens to provide a local source of compost and foster community involvement.

-Shared Resources: Pool resources and knowledge to create more efficient and productive worm farming systems.

-Non-Profit and Social Enterprises:

-Social Impact: Develop worm farming projects aimed at reducing food waste and promoting sustainable agriculture practices within communities.

-Employment Opportunities: Create job opportunities in urban and rural areas through community-based worm farming enterprises.

-Municipal Support:

-Government Initiatives: Encourage municipalities to support and fund worm farming projects as part of their waste management and sustainability programs.

-Policy Development: Advocate for policies that promote composting and organic waste diversion at the local and regional levels.

CHAPTER TWELVE

CASE STUDIES AND SUCCESS STORIES

12.1 Profiles of Successful Worm Farmers

-John Peterson, The Urban Vermiculturist:

  -Background: Started with a small apartment worm bin, now runs a large-scale urban vermiculture business.

  -Key Achievements: Developed efficient systems for indoor and rooftop worm farming, supplies organic fertilizer to local urban farms and gardens.

  -Advice: "Start small and perfect your techniques. Pay close attention to your worms' needs and be patient."

-Sara Lopez, The Community Advocate:

  -Background: Initiated a community-based worm farming project in a suburban neighborhood.

  -Key Achievements: Transformed local organic waste into valuable compost for community gardens, educated hundreds on sustainable practices.

-Advice: "Involve the community and educate. Worm farming can be a powerful tool for environmental stewardship and community building."

-Mike Brown, The Agricultural Innovator:

-Background: Integrated worm farming into his large-scale organic farm, focusing on soil health and sustainability.

-Key Achievements: Improved crop yields and soil fertility, reduced chemical fertilizer use by 75%.

-Advice: "Understand the science behind worm farming. Healthy soil is the foundation of successful agriculture."

-Emily Chen, The Entrepreneur:

-Background: Founded a successful e-commerce business selling worm castings, compost tea, and live worms.

-Key Achievements: Grew a small hobby into a profitable enterprise with national reach.

-Advice: "Focus on quality and customer education. Building a trustworthy brand is crucial for long-term success."

12.2 Lessons Learned from Real-life Experiences

- Adapting to Challenges:

-Overcoming Environmental Issues: Many successful worm farmers emphasize the importance of monitoring and adjusting environmental conditions to keep worms healthy.

-Case Study: John Peterson had to develop innovative solutions to keep his rooftop worm farms cool during hot summer months, such as using reflective covers and increasing bin ventilation.

-Effective Marketing Strategies:

-Building a Brand: Successful farmers like Emily Chen highlight the importance of branding and customer education to differentiate their products in the market.

-Case Study: Sara Lopez's community project gained traction by hosting workshops and demonstrations, creating a strong local following and demand for her products.

- Community Engagement:

-Creating Impactful Projects: Engaging the local community can lead to broader success and support for worm farming initiatives.

-Case Study: Sara Lopez's community-based approach not only managed local organic waste but also fostered a sense of community ownership and responsibility towards sustainable practices.

-Innovations and Experimentation:

-Continuous Improvement: Experimenting with different methods and systems can lead to significant improvements in efficiency and output.

-Case Study: Mike Brown continuously tests new bedding materials and feeding regimens to optimize worm health and casting production, resulting in better crop yields.

-Financial Management:

-Sustainable Growth: Managing finances wisely is crucial for scaling up operations and ensuring long-term sustainability.

-Case Study: Emily Chen managed her growth by reinvesting profits into expanding her product line and improving her production facilities, ensuring sustainable business growth.

-Educational Outreach:

-Spreading Knowledge: Sharing knowledge through workshops, online content, and community involvement helps build a supportive network and customer base.

-Case Study: John Peterson frequently collaborates with local schools and urban farming programs to teach vermiculture, creating future generations of environmentally conscious individuals.

CHAPTER THIRTEEN

RESOURCES AND FURTHER READING

13.1 Recommended Books and Websites

- Books:

-"Worms Eat My Garbage" by Mary Appelhof: A classic guide on vermiculture, perfect for beginners and experienced worm farmers.

-"The Worm Farmer's Handbook: Mid- to Large-Scale Vermicomposting for Farms, Businesses, Municipalities, Schools, and Institutions" by Rhonda Sherman: Comprehensive resource for scaling up worm farming operations.

-"Vermiculture Technology: Earthworms, Organic Wastes, and Environmental Management" edited by Clive A. Edwards, Norman Q. Arancon, and Rhonda Sherman: In-depth academic resource covering the science and applications of vermiculture.

-"The Complete Guide to Working with Worms: Using the Gardener's Best Friend for Organic Gardening and Composting" by Wendy M. Vincent: Practical advice on integrating worm farming into gardening practices.

-"Worm Farming Revolution: Your Guide to Setting Up and Operating a Successful Worm Farming Business" by Taylor Reed: A practical guide for those looking to turn worm farming into a business.

-Websites:

-Red Worm Composting (www.redwormcomposting.com): Offers tutorials, tips, and a community forum for vermiculture enthusiasts.

-Vermiculture.com (www.vermiculture.com): Resource hub with articles, research papers, and product reviews related to worm farming.

-Worm Farming Secrets (www.wormfarmingsecrets.com): Subscription-based service providing newsletters and expert advice on worm farming.

-The Worm Guide (www.thewormguide.com): Comprehensive guide with step-by-step instructions and troubleshooting tips.

-Urban Worm Company (www.urbanwormcompany.com): Blog and store offering products and advice for urban worm farming.

13.2 Organizations and Associations

-North America:

-Vermiculture Institute: Provides education, research, and resources for worm farmers across North America.

-U.S. Composting Council: Organization dedicated to the development, expansion, and promotion of the composting industry, including vermiculture.

-Vermiculture Society of America: Network of vermiculture enthusiasts and professionals sharing knowledge and best practices.

-International:

-International Vermicomposting Network: Global network promoting vermicomposting practices and research.

-European Compost Network: Promotes composting and vermiculture practices across Europe.

-Worm Farming Alliance: International association offering support and resources for commercial worm farmers.

-Local and Regional:

-Local Extension Services: Many agricultural extension services offer resources and support for vermiculture.

-Community Gardening Groups: Often have members experienced in vermiculture who can provide advice and support.

-Environmental NGOs: Many environmental organizations support vermiculture as part of their sustainability initiatives.

13.3 Glossary of Terms

-Aeration: The process of introducing air into the composting system to maintain aerobic conditions.

-Bedding: Materials used in worm bins to provide a habitat for worms, such as shredded newspaper, cardboard, or coconut coir.

-Castings: The nutrient-rich excrement produced by composting worms, also known as vermicast or worm manure.

-Compost Tea: A liquid fertilizer made by steeping worm castings in water to extract nutrients and beneficial microorganisms.

- Continuous Flow-Through System: A type of worm bin design that allows for the continuous harvesting of worm castings from the bottom while fresh waste is added on top.

- Feedstock: Organic material provided as food for worms, including kitchen scraps and garden waste.

- Leachate: Liquid that drains from a compost pile or worm bin, which can be rich in nutrients but may also contain harmful substances if not properly managed.

- Microorganisms: Tiny living organisms, such as bacteria and fungi, that play a crucial role in the decomposition process.

- pH: A measure of acidity or alkalinity, important for maintaining a healthy worm bin environment.

- Vermiculture: The cultivation of worms for the purpose of composting organic waste and producing worm castings.

- Vermicomposting: The process of using worms to convert organic waste into nutrient-rich compost.

CHAPTER FOURTEEN

APPENDICES

14.1 Frequently Asked Questions (FAQ)

- How do I start a worm farm?

-Answer: Begin by selecting a suitable worm bin, preparing the bedding, sourcing composting worms (typically red wigglers), and adding your organic waste. Maintain optimal moisture, temperature, and aeration conditions.

- What can I feed my worms?

-Answer: Worms can eat most organic kitchen scraps such as fruit and vegetable peels, coffee grounds, and tea bags. Avoid feeding them meat, dairy, oily foods, and acidic items like citrus.

-How often should I feed my worms?

-Answer: Feed your worms a small amount of food once a week and adjust based on how quickly they consume it. Overfeeding can lead to odor problems and attract pests.

-How do I maintain the moisture level in my worm bin?

-Answer: The bedding should be as moist as a wrung-out sponge. Add water if it is too dry or mix in dry bedding materials if it is too wet.

- What do I do if my worm bin starts to smell?

-Answer: Bad odors are usually a sign of overfeeding or poor aeration. Reduce the amount of food, mix in dry bedding, and ensure the bin is well-ventilated.

-How do I harvest worm castings?

-Answer: Harvest castings by pushing all contents to one side of the bin and adding fresh bedding and food to the other. Worms will migrate to the new side, allowing you to collect the castings. Alternatively, use a continuous flow-through system.

-What do I do if pests invade my worm bin?

-Answer: Identify the pest and adjust bin conditions accordingly. For fruit flies, ensure food is buried under bedding. For ants, maintain proper moisture levels. For mites, balance the bin's moisture and reduce acidic foods.

-Can I keep my worm bin outside?

-Answer: Yes, but you must protect it from extreme temperatures. Insulate the bin in cold weather and provide shade in hot weather. Ensure it is secure from predators and pests.

14.2 Templates and Record-Keeping Forms

-Feeding Log Template:

-Date:

-Food Added:

-Quantity:

-Observations (e.g., worm activity, uneaten food):

-Next Feeding Date:

-Moisture and Temperature Log Template:

-Date:

-Moisture Level:

-Temperature:

-Adjustments Made (e.g., added water, moved bin):

-Harvesting Log Template:

  -Date of Harvest:

  -Amount of Castings Collected:

  -Method Used:

  -Observations (e.g., worm health, bin conditions):

-Sales and Inventory Record Template:

  -Date:

  -Product Sold (e.g., worm castings, live worms):

  -Quantity:

  -Price:

  -Customer Information:

  -Inventory Balance:

14.3 Supplier Directory

-Worm Suppliers:

  -Uncle Jim's Worm Farm: Offers red wigglers, European nightcrawlers, and worm farming supplies.

-The Worm Dude: Specializes in composting worms and worm bin accessories.

-Worms 4 Earth: Provides a variety of composting worms and educational materials.

-Worm Bin Suppliers:

-The Urban Worm Company: Sells continuous flow-through worm bins and related products.

-VermiHut: Offers multi-layered worm composting systems.

-Nature's Footprint: Known for their Worm Factory series of worm bins.

-Bedding and Feed Suppliers:

-Coconut Coir: Available at garden centers and online retailers like Amazon.

-Shredded Paper: Local office supply stores or recycling centers.

-Peat Moss: Found at home improvement stores and garden centers.

-Composting Supplies:

-Compost Thermometers: Available from garden supply stores and online retailers.

-pH Meters: Available from agricultural supply stores and online retailers.

-Moisture Meters: Found at garden centers and home improvement stores.

CHAPTER FIFTEEN

INDEX

A

- Aeration: 5.3, 10.1

- Anatomy of Worms: 2.2

- Aquaponics Integration: 8.3

B

- Bedding:

  - Choosing Bedding: 3.2

  - Managing Bedding: 5.4

- Behavior of Worms: 2.3

- Breeding Worms: 7.1

C

- Castings:

  - Harvesting: 6.1, 6.2

- Using: 6.3

- Community Initiatives: 11.3

- Compost Tea: 9.3

- Continuous Flow-Through System: 13.3

D

- Diversifying Products: 9.3

E

- Environmental Benefits: 11.1

- Expanding Worm Farm: 7.3

F

- Feeding:

  - What to Feed: 4.1

  - Foods to Avoid: 4.2

  - Feeding Schedule: 4.3

  - Managing Food Waste: 4.4

- Fertilizer: See Castings

G

- Glossary: 13.3

H

- Harvesting:

  - When to Harvest: 6.1

  - Methods: 6.2

I

- Indoor Farming: 8.1

L

- Life Cycle of Worms: 2.3

- Lessons from Experts: 12.2

M

- Managing Population: 7.2

- Marketing Castings: 9.2

- Moisture Levels: 5.1

N

- Nutrient-Rich Castings: See Castings

O

- Optimal Conditions: 3.4

- Organizations: 13.2

- Outdoor Farming: 8.1

- Overview of Worm Farming: 1.3

P

- Pest Control: 5.4, 10.1

- Preventing Failures: 10.2

- Profiles of Worm Farmers: 12.1

R

- Record-Keeping Forms: 14.2

- Reducing Landfill Waste: 11.1

S

- Scaling Up: 9.1

- Soil Health: 11.1

- Storing Castings: 6.3

- Sustainable Waste Management: 11.2

- Supplier Directory: 14.3

T

- Temperature Control: 5.2

- Troubleshooting: 10.1

- Types of Worms: 2.1

V

- Vermiculture Technology: See Glossary

- Ventilation: 5.3

W

- Waste Management: 11.2

- Websites: 13.1

- Worm Bins:

  - Choosing: 3.1

  - Types: 13.3

- Worm Behavior: 2.3

- Worm Towers: 8.2

- Worm Tea: 9.3

Y

- Yields: See Harvesting.

THANKS FOR READING

www.ingramcontent.com/pod-product-compliance
Lightning Source LLC
Chambersburg PA
CBHW050236230526
45470CB00005B/1987